THE DAY BEF(

Praise for MOTHER, NATURE

'There are poems in this collection that knocked me clean to the
ground, as others offered me a warm hand up and others still,
which stroked my backbone as I sobbed. The subject is crucial,
but it's the beauty of the poems which holds it all together.'
— HOLLIE McNISH

'Aoife Lyall's *Mother, Nature* is a beautiful and moving
collection – a fine debut.' – MICHAEL LONGLEY

'One of Lyall's most effective techniques is the exploration
of paradox [...] which makes the best poems here particularly
devastating in their contained forms.'
— SEÁN HEWITT, *The Irish Times*

'Aoife Lyall's collection *Mother, Nature* arrives with a magisterial
maturity that belies its status as a first book-length offering...
A remarkable debut from a strong talent.'
— ÉAMON MAG UIDHIR, *Dublin Review of Books*

'*Mother, Nature* by Aoife Lyall was an incredibly powerful book.
[...] I found myself blown away by the visceral nature of the writing.'
— VINCENT LAL, Co-Judge, Scottish First Book Award

'This collection does important work to break silences and stigma,
and delves into motherhood with depth, complexity and nuance.'
— JULIE MORRISSY, *Poetry Ireland Review*

'The capacity of language to convey the intensity of the most
human moments is explored with an unusual combination of
directness and gentleness in Aoife Lyall's startling debut, *Mother,
Nature*.[...] This is a strong first collection, rich as a newborn
with promise.' — ELIZABETH RIDOUT, *Agenda*

Aoife Lyall (née Griffin) was born in Dublin in 1987. She earned her BA in English Studies from Trinity College Dublin, before reading her MPhil in Medieval Literature at St John's, University of Cambridge, and gaining her PGDE (English) at the University of Aberdeen. She was awarded an Emerging Scottish Writer residency by Cove Park in 2020 and was twice shortlisted for the Hennessy New Irish Writing Awards. Her poems have also been shortlisted in the Wells Festival of Literature Open Poetry Competition and the Jane Martin Poetry Prize.

Her first collection, *Mother, Nature*, was published by Bloodaxe Books in 2021 and was shortlisted for the Scottish First Book Award, one of Scotland's National Book Awards 2021. Her second collection, *The Day Before*, followed from Bloodaxe in 2024, supported by The National Lottery through Creative Scotland's Open Fund. She is reviews editor of *Magma Poetry*, and has worked for the Scottish Poetry Library as a mentor and curator, the Saltire Society as a judge, and *Butcher's Dog* as a guest editor. Her poems have inspired music, film, sculpture and artwork across the UK and Ireland. She lives and works in the Scottish Highlands with her family.

AOIFE LYALL

The Day Before

BLOODAXE BOOKS

ISBN: 978 1 78037 690 5

First published 2024 by
Bloodaxe Books Ltd,
Eastburn,
South Park,
Hexham,
Northumberland NE46 1BS.

www.bloodaxebooks.com
For further information about Bloodaxe titles
please visit our website and join our mailing list
or write to the above address for a catalogue.

Cover design: Neil Astley & Pamela Robertson-Pearce

Printed in Great Britain by Bell & Bain Limited, Glasgow, Scotland, on
acid-free paper sourced from mills with FSC chain of custody certification.

CONTENTS

For you, for me, for us, for them

The day before

We go to the homewares store.
It has a café.

We comment on the tiger lamp, the nautical clock,
the sheepskin rug.

When I walk through the aisle of mirrors,
each one grabs

a piece of me for itself. Limbs savaged
from my torso

head nowhere to be found, I find frames
for paintings waiting

to be hung and glasses to replace the ones
we clean until they crack.

The early shift

Towels loll out of drawers like grotesque
        tongues and oven gloves hang hollow by the thumbs.

Squash skins decompose by the sink's stagnant
        steeping water, and the bin bag stinks with human waste.

I shatter breadsticks like blanched bones, step over
        the bruised flesh of discarded bananas.

Harlequined animals, undisturbed by my incautious route, gaze up
        in a kaleidoscope of awkward angles

at the curls of pork fat unfurling in the morning sun –
        the pink lilies of an insatiable lover.

Matinee

I talk to you – like any mother would –
about our trip away, the empty fridge,
what to have for dinner, a script I run

from aisle to aisle, full of imminent
birthdays, phantom guests. (*Flour. Sugar.
Loo roll. Eggs.*) You watch my words,

mirror my lips. (*Packet. Pasta. Sachet. Dried.*)
I make a show of forgetting, going back.
(*Noodles. Herbs. Long-life milk. Things*

in jars, preserved in oils or spices.) I plan
what to leave behind, when I will return.
(*Sweet things that will keep. And soap. And soap.*)

Moss

We thought it was pen at first or paint, a dab
under the chin, worked under the nails, found

in the folds of elbows, the backs of knees. But no.
We have started to moss. We see it everywhere:

the woods, the parks, the playgrounds; parents
trying to hide it under hats and gloves, children

picking it off each other like scabs. Some compare
colours, trace the lines as islands join to islands

form their soft continents. Advice arrives on the wind
like spores *use less water, get more sunlight, consider*

introducing competitive plants. We steer clear of sulfates,
scrub at it in the bath and shower, swap our sheets

for sand and gravel, but still it comes. And soon we start
to see whole families covered in the stuff. They move

slowly, erratic, glacial, curl up under slides and seesaws,
become benchmarks and bollards, milestones

and street sculptures, until those in charge are forced
to admit to the rest of us, all hanging by a thread –

Essential items

I wouldn't have you see this for the world:
green crates starved of vegetation; the sunken
bones of white shelves picked clean. A single pallet,
stranded in the central aisle. I circle it like a shark,
tear through cellophane as tough and supple as cartilage.

Scavenger fish, my hands dart in and out for tins
of chopped tomatoes, pinto beans. I leave,
one small bag full; the other half-hidden like shame.
Tethered to the heavens, you point behind me. *The flowers!*
you call, *The Easter eggs!* Angled around the exit, they keep
the secret of my ocean heart, tide my aching fists.

Torch

for Piano

Composed by Jake Morgan

Inspired by the poem *'Torch'* by Aoife Lyall
from **The Day Before** (Bloodaxe Books, 2024)

Torch

A small thing, with coloured discs that slip
between the light and lens, it projects a host

of carnivores across our doors and walls. Until
one frame is just – an eye – big enough to dream.

I make a trick of hiding it, and leave a moon
for you to swell and shrink with insatiable orbit.

Determined to explore the deepest corners
of our makeshift den, you discover lost worlds

behind the curtains, figures fossilised in dust,
their shadows moon-dark beside missing bricks

and bits of breakfast, feral socks and stickers
with the mass and magnitude of asteroids.

And behind the couch, full of stars and covered
in dust, a yellow balloon, silent now and small,

knowing it was born from the dust the light
is dancing for: that it too was once a star.

Hamper

There is no wicker here, or straw – no delicacies
or dainty preserves – just cardboard boxes and plastic
bags filled with the dinner meat and breakfast butter,
the buffet fruit, the bread for afternoon tea. I collect it

from a local hotel – the one past the crematorium
where every other car turns off – and do what I am told to do –
Do not arrive too early or too late. Reverse

into the pick-up bay and wait. Someone masked
and gloved will fill your boot with the food
you ordered at least three days ago. We do not
speak or touch – *Keep your windows up* – or get close
enough to see each other's eyes.

I like to think her eyes are green – with flecks of grey
that flicker blue when she drives home by the loch –
I like to think that someone knows for sure.

Mortification of the flesh

Slow-cooked sauce so thick it sits in the bowl of a perforated spoon.
We drain the pasta, grate the cheese, haul the linguine from colander
to coloured plates and call you through. Wrapped round the plastic tines
you mouth, and hold, and pull the pasta through pursed lips, sluicing off
the meat and sauce and cheese until, mouth full, you bite.
It slips, in slow motion, down your chin, falls to your chest, collapses
in a heap by your upright, pious knees. A trail of bloodied welts marks
your vest, rings your thighs like a chain cilice. Unaware of the splatters,
indifferent to the stains, your stomach is nothing more than something
to be filled, from your plate or mine, and when you are done, we strip you
bare, run a bath, sponge the rusted dinner from your hair, your face,
your feet, from in-between your fingers and underneath your chin. Sanctified,
asleep, we deny ourselves the comfort of the couch, begin our easy penance:
clean the table, soak the clothes, kneel to pick the pasta off the floor.

The Hail Mary box

Under the spare bed in the spare room – hidden behind cardboard crates filled with books, notes, planners, diaries, tour guides and newspapers – the supplies lie face down and keep quiet. Ready for my last breath, or his, or the empty cupboards of a desperate kitchen, that box is full of grace. And lentils, rice, a jar of olive oil, a tin each of peaches, chopped tomatoes, baked beans – pineapple chunks that will stay uneaten even then. No flour yet, but long-life milk and herbs, stock cubes, tins of tuna, tubes of paste, pasta and couscous in one kilo bags. And underneath, a single Dairy Milk, its purple wrapper full of promise, penance, sacrifice.

Bath night

I worry the dry skin on your scalp with lathered fingers

tilt your chin and rinse the suds away

                                   just like my mother

but she was quicker than this, nails firmer too.

       Love so fierce it could hurt.

                             Her left hand held to my forehead

                             like a prophet,

her right its weekly baptism.

                       Hair wet, hip hoisted,

I pull the plug and drain the Irish sea.

                                 Boats moored, planes grounded

I carry you across the reclaimed land: set you by the fire

                            she keeps burning through the night.

In bits

They number in their thousands – squares, rectangles, blanks, and flats –
gathered from every toy box, every drawer, every top shelf in this house.
And when there are not enough, we order more. The kits gift us special parts –
fulcrums, doorways, levers, discs – rods for chassis and curtain poles, for telescopes
and torpedoes. For weeks we build the places we cannot go – cities and cinemas,
theatres and zoos. Opaque, translucent, uncanny or nothing like – we fill them all
with people.

        And then, smaller. Our favourite places, the local park – its static
swings and chunky slides, its non-plussed ducks – no, too much now, too many.
It comes down to this –

        two friends in a café on the kitchen windowsill
sitting on their plastic chairs, coffee cups the only thing

        between them, talking
about the cousin's dog, the latest show – the whole thing unremarkable.
Just there, together,

        smiles so wide they could be painted on.

The big shop

Mute, alone, we wander to the back of the queue, start
to wait. Some of us have lists but we are all beggars here.
The trolleys start and stop, and start and stop and finally

I make it to the top, wipe and wash and wait for instructions:
which arrows I must follow, which precautions I must take
which products are limited so each person has a chance.

And after all that, there is nothing – produce, yes, rows
and rows of it, haunted by people who can't commit
themselves to what others may have touched. But there

are no newborns here, curlicued into cotton slings
as their parents rock the trolley, soothe the squash,
figure out what formula they'd need and if to buy it.

There are no toddlers pushing trollies or prostrate
on the floor, or slung over shoulders yelling protests
and demands the rest of us can hear but cannot meet.

No eager queue at the pizza counter, or tiptoed noses
peering over to where the heaps and mounds of toppings
used to be, no teddy bears on tour before returning

to their shelf. No chorus of entreaties for sweeties
and the silence that comes with them, no final requests
or closing arguments in the push towards the tills,

no babies on conveyor belts or sports teams packing bags,
or crisps sneakily being opened or hands waiting for their tokens,
no melted hearts or frazzled nerves – just a big shop.

My Scottish fathers

I see them everywhere –

In black trousers that dip at the waist, pool at the ankles
in short-sleeved check shirts and faded straw hats.

Their forearms are thick and tanned with garden sun
their feet more shuffle now than stride but sure

enough to go for miles through the flashes of uncertainty
forked by changing shop fronts, one-way streets.

Bearded, bare-faced, bald or crowned with silver thorns –
each of them missing something in their own way.

(Me.
I hope it's me.)

The train

You peer over his shoulder and under his arm, impatient
for the train that will carry us to London, Edinburgh,

America, Australia, the moon. On my knees, I coax you
to sit on the kitchen chairs lined up against the wall.

Coats on, hats in hand, we wait as he conducts the final
checks: scrutinises the sidings, the signals, the footbridge,

makes the line secure. And then the train arrives, plucked
from the plumes of tissue paper it sends into the sky.

A steam train, all red and black, he sets it on the tiny track,
so we can see it go, hear the *clicka-clacka-clicka-clacka-click*

clicka-clacka-clicka-clacka-click, clicka-clacka-clicka-clacka click
He asks for the tickets we spent the morning making

and we step across the yellow lines I painted on the floor.
We spend all afternoon on that train and oh the places we go

and the people we see, with our tinfoil sandwiches and cups
of juice, until it is time for dinner and bath and bed. And then

we sit, too weary now to make-believe without you, and we
watch the train speed round and round its tiny track. Too big

and too small to leave out overnight, we put it away,
shake the coal dust from our hair before we go to sleep.

rainbow

dripping in dragon's blood, vermilion, rosso corsa, I prise the lids
off paint tins full of amber, ginger, saffron. I use whatever
I can find – paintbrushes, rollers, mops, rags – to spread the colours
thick and fast across the doors and walls, the fence, the sky in an arc
of shifting ladders, aching limbs. Before the thirty-two shades of home
dashes of Van Gogh yellow finish the fire, followed by the blues
all lapis lazuli and jazz to sing you through the hazy indigo of another
nightmare shift. I crush idle amethysts to dust, martyr the front door.

Going in circles

You play with the rotary washing-line
grasping the corner of the duvet in each fist

walking it around like a mule at a millstone.
With every revolution he exclaims *my jacket*

my jacket the green gilet drip-drying on the line
wet with the water from a bucket full of stones.

And you walk and he jumps and I wait until
all of us are crying and none of us knows why.

Traffic calming

Strapped into your car seat, you settle to Purcell's *Close thine eyes*
    and sleep secure as your father sways the car through chicanes and kerb
        extensions. He halts at junctions and give ways, keeps time
            with the rain and the wipers, flicks his wrists to indicate
        a slow, a turn, a pause to let another driver in. And I think
    of all the others, the lines of traffic composed of cars the country over, filled with
restless babies, the hearts of a million parents,
    or two, turned to the DJ as they hold the silver tune in their mouths
        and drive on, and on again, the indelible rhythm
            tongue-written on their teeth.

Sundays

They're all there – the slippers, the walking boots, the modest brogues,
two pairs of well-worn runners, the black soft-soled slip-ons,
the suede sandals and the high heels, and then the three pairs of Uggs,
in gold, concrete, and sand, lined, unlined, and trimmed with fur – all listening
to the easy laughter wafting from the kitchen with the smell of cooked ham
and parsley sauce, with the clatter of plates pushed too close together,
the news of cars and jobs, of family plans and future friends, all floating
into the hall together, where all those shoes lie piled and pushed together
by the door. And I am standing on the doorstep. Waiting. Waiting. Waiting.

Wildflowers

(for my husband, on our tenth wedding anniversary)

They grow in fits and starts – scattered from a spare box you unearthed
in the garage – out of the soil you destoned for months, and sieved
and nourished with compost and topsoil you mixed by hand. At first

we do not know if they will grow, or what is weed or flower, or when
to give them water or how they will survive. Then other things need doing
and still they burst through and bloom and still we call them *wildflowers*

the way we say *love* to mean petals, pollen, stamen, seed. You pick them
for me, for our anniversary, and your wild abandon fills the crystal vases
we were given all those years ago. Up close you marvel at the variety

of the flowers, the complexities of their form, at their ability to grow
and yet to know, to say *they would not be here if not for us*. I look to our
children, flowers stirring in their roots, our love in their wild hearts.

Suburban soundscape: Summer

the gentle discord of the dutiful homebound driving by in droves; the neighbours sharing their news and views and easy laughter in gardens just inches from our own; friends saying their goodbyes at the door, beeping their horns to the thumping clunk and wallop of side gates and bins and bikes flung into garages and sheds; the twilight roar of hedge trimmers and lawnmowers; the bone shiver of a stubborn shovel on stone, the scattering of bark, the hiss and spit of sprinklers and then – there it is! The muffled rock and pop, the hard metal that tells us dinner has arrived in cars laden with pizza, curry, fish and chips for this postcode and the next and next. And, in every house, the silent rush of parents vaulting over furniture, getting to the hall before the doorbell rings, before the driver knocks, calls out *hello*, and wakes the children just asleep – martyred for their efforts, the same time every week.

A day at the beach

You build sandcastles, sifting through sand
and stones for a favourite you have yet to find.
I sit here, shelling out sun cream and sandwiches,
palming the dry sand like a duvet, feeling it fold
and unfold over my fingers, fingers that stack stones
like dinner plates and breakfast bowls and – since
we have the weather for it – string up some seaweed
and hang the sea-spun tumbled towels to dry.
All too soon, it is time for us to go. I scrub the sand
from your body with froth and salt. We have one last
look for mermaid's purses, missing keys; leave behind
a lonely rockpool, left to soak: its steep edges crusted
with porcelain crabs, its forgotten shallows full of fish.

Maternal instinct

The late summer sun casts them all
in chiaroscuro, stills them as they crouch
and crowd around the neighbour's dog.

A homely tableau, you stand in the shadow
of our house, watching, working out
where and when and how to be a part of it

until I cannot bear it. I hand you a scalpel
tell you *Open my heart instead. Show them*
the beating fist of it: your name on every knuckle.

Phantom

No one comments on the absence –
indifferent perhaps, or afraid of appearing
indiscreet. So, it's business as usual: codes

for the photocopier, cash for the kitty, chip
in for the flowers for somebody's something,
scrub a dozen coffee cups left to mould.

The pain starts just below my elbow –
where you should sit and twist until the sinews
clutch the tendons to the edge of worn-out bone.

There's nothing for it now but work. I peer
inside the empty mug – for cracks, for signs
of strain – but my heart just isn't in it.

Day trip

Tickets booked well in advance, we arrive in good time to beat
the queue, follow the signs to the makeshift entrance booth.
The man who bars our way is surly, tired. It is early autumn

and he has manned this station all summer long. His script
is short, perfunctory, precise. The paperwork lies heavy
in a lap full of reservations, photo IDs, our proof of address.

There are no concessions here – we will not pay with cash or card
but hard-earned spit and tears. We put on a good show for you,
make a game of counting the cones that narrow the road and stop

us turning back. Pretend the car is on a track, and the rows of ramps
are something to delight in, like the lights and lines and signs
that lead us to marquees set up like market stalls. They wave us in

and smile like automatons, waiting for the car to hit its mark
so they can speak and hold up signs and slip things through the window.
And we can play along – talk through phones like walkie-talkies, treat

the testing packs like party bags (a bag of buttons slipped inside
to make something more of yours than tissue, paper, swab – until
we reverse into the testing station, and they tell us to begin.

Artisan

You have the wind in your hair. The sun
shines through the intricate warp and weft
of it, the filigree and fretwork of a day
already passing. In my element, I listen
to the myths the wind has woven into you –
unpick its stitches, unspin its yarn, release
the tips of tails from the mouths of snakes –
brush your hair to burnished gold, wonder
what the wind will make of you tomorrow.

Psithuros

You will not sleep, so I sing you a world
of plants and flowers, fields and rivers. I sing

until the trees grow up around me, until my toes
gnarl and knuckle to the floor. I sing until

the words transpire from my throat, flow over
chapped lips, crack like bark. I sing until the rings

of recitation grow and tighten like drought, until
my body sways in the breeze of the only song

that will settle you. I sing until you are sound asleep
and listen to your breath, hushing through the leaves.

Chaos

The darkness before there is light or sky
to hold it – when there are no shadows

because there is no sun to cast them
no land for them to land on – when the sea

does not move because there is no moon
to move for and the stars are nothing more

than pencil marks on plans – when the world
is filled with plants and trees unmade

with no wind yet to shake or spread them –
when the animals of land and sea and sky wait

inside our books and songs and hands and we
the masters of them all. Soon there will be light

but, for now, all is quiet, and all is well and I
the only one awake in this, our almost universe –

Snow poem

I spend days looking for it
in snow drifts and weighted
branches, in the pawprints
of dogs, in the ridges
of the
neighbours' boots
in the snowman I repurpose
as a clay horse and cast in bronze
like a hand or a foot
in the
hushing rush of a steam train
coupling and uncoupling, conjured
from a sled pulled over shallow snow.
Until there it is, the
poem
I have been waiting for
falling between the open boot
and the front door, falling onto
your upturned palm, your skyward tongue.

Day Return

They wander the streets with me, searching
for a steering wheel, a trolley, a pram, a hand.

I give them the edge of my scarf, the belt
on my coat, the button on my lapel, stuff them
in my pockets to burrow in the debris of home

receipts from that new old-fashioned sweet shop
wet wipes used for sticky fingers or muddy hands
tags from new toys, tickets, coins. But it is no use.

Skin cracked, knuckles raw, fingertips barbed
like fishhooks from bottles plunged and scrubbed
in scalding water, my hands will not rest until

I give them something to do. So I buy them
a keychain teddy bear and tell them it's for you.

Tow Path

There is a crow on the tow path, dipping its beak
in and out, and in and out of a shattered blue egg.

Its beak is slathered in yolk, yolk that yellows
the ground like gorse. It stops. And it watches me.

Miles from home, I want to turn back. This is not
a straight path or a narrow one, but there is no other way

of living. If I leave now, that egg will follow me home
and I will sit on it for days until it hatches into something

else that is not mine. So I walk on, cross and cross over
the lock, until it is all forgotten: the crow full or frightened

away by families, friends, or tourists; the shell crushed
or pushed into the grass; the yolk scuffed, gently, with dust.

The back of five

I

The third – or fourth – awakening: third – or fourth –
iteration of a baby for whom deprivation is less than womb.

> Bleary eyes blink awake to stained sheets still sweating,
> stir fingers and tongue to fumble and mumble through leaking
> and changing to

– latch –

the ache that spreads from the taut elastic
of a lower back, now propped against pillows
that barely slept between my knees
three days ago.

> Where desire bucked and raged pain
> holds me to the bed with a gravity that forgoes
> the nursing chair in the baby's room,

surrounded by boxes, balanced against superstitions
in an impossible place, full of time and distance
I cannot comprehend.

II

A missed step and this is the closest to the floor you have ever been.
Held in arms so carefully, so firmly, you are nothing more than curious
about this new and sudden view.

                                    It will be weeks before you find yourself
on a mottled playmat looking up at faces that orbit yours like moons –
parts of you that spun and crashed together, that formed you in their atmosphere.

Almost always not fully asleep, I watch the floppy-haired, wide-smiled scientist.
He walks on Mercury in an *eternal twilight*, thinks he knows what that feels like,
thinks he can tell us how the universe works,

                                              when he doesn't know this television
is a star in the galaxy of new mothers, millions of us who have never known
such darkness, seen such light.

III

Bottles and breadsticks on the concession stand of the kitchen counter,
we queue by the kettle, wait for the boil and cool, shuffle to our seats
in the apologetic dusk, determined to ignore the stickiness on the floor,
along the armrest, the stale food going soft beneath my feet. We watch
the trailers together and by the time the main feature starts you are calm,
your body moulded into the cushion of my stomach for the railway children,
the orient express, the great expectations of pride and prejudice; for die-hard
explorers, intrepid New Yorkers, happy princes and great Gatsbys, consulting
detectives with their despairing clientele, planets swirling blue, green and frozen.
Together, we travel from Paris to Punxsutawney, from the world wars to galaxies
far far away, from new worlds to old worlds to other worlds. We learn the human
heart is full of stardust and acorns and dinosaurs, that the heart is subject to –
and capable of – great change: that few people are without one or miss a chance
to use it. And as trains whistle, confetti flutters, couples lean in for the kiss,
sunlight slips through the dawn curtains and I carry you upstairs.

IV

Little composer, practised orchestrator, you conduct us
from the podium of your cot. Left palm pressed
        to the pillow, my practiced breath keeps time
        with the swaddled batons of your legs, determined
to counter the lift and drop of your father's affected
shoulders. When you point to me, hand cupped and dropped,
        I thrill with a practised start, lie still to rise and better rise
        with your next stirring. Martyr of the early start, I devote
myself to the subtleties of your character, the nuances of your form,
the effort to make us understand it is you who knows the score.

V

You march on the family bed
       (that is what it is called now,
       not the *now* of the poem but the now of its writing)

and knowing how to stand up for yourself
you stand
tall
against
the
headboard

square up to a mirrored wardrobe
that leaves us always outnumbered.

You watch your arms stretch, your knees
bend: we watch for gravity, brace for landing.

Then the pit-pat pit-pat of your sister
       (with whom I started this poem but who
       aged out of it when I wasn't looking)

and the air is filled with the launch and flight,
the fall and muffled landing of pandas, tigers, huskies,

a bewildered octopus. When she climbs aboard
we find ourselves no longer under siege but at sea,

            adrift, the four of us

        (suddenly inevitably and always a four)

          awash in breath and laughter
           for an entire moment

VI

The unsettled shadows speak for you, morning spirit
who floats into the family bed and waits for me to furl
and unfurl the bedding around us. You fall asleep
      in the foetal position, knees pushed against my back
      where wings would grow so I go, and make my way
      past the painted lovers kissing on the turret stairs
            past piles of waiting toys and wet washing
            to your still-warm bed, your sheets a night sky
            full of stars, the night sky filled with dancing light.

VII

We are in the sea, the three of us.
I brought you here myself.
Confident I can keep you safe,
we laugh for a time, splash, swim.

Then you both go under.
And I have to choose.
I choose you: you I find later.

When I wake a second time,
not grasping at the sheets like surf,
you are asleep beside me: your cheek
just as soft, but not nearly so cold.

VIII

Stripped sheets and fresh pyjamas,
we sneak downstairs to the sound
of your dreams, look at picture books,
read stories until the heating kicks in
and makes it warm enough for counting
and colouring at the kitchen table.

    Coffee still too loud to contemplate,
ours is the quiet play of puzzles
and playdough and sand, of making
lists, making plans, making breakfast,
getting dressed, taking requests for what
you want to watch with me
while the others are asleep.

    And when we sit beside each other
eating the porridge I have cooked
and cooled, stirred and served with swirls
of chocolate chips, you turn to me and smile
and wave a little, as if we have just met.

    As if this is the first time we have been here,
like this, just the two of us together, in the almost morning,

*   *   *

Knuckles

As accurate and imprecise as a month of ligaments
I cast my mother's knuckles in bronze – use them

to bunch the legs of capricious tights and socks,
to hold a halo of fabric around my daughter's feet,

stretch them to her chest, her chin – tendons designed
to test the toes of shoes, the waistbands of jeans.

When in doubt, I knead them into the runed skin
of my hollow chest. Hold up the mirror. Read.

Big School

Wary yet eager to impress on their first day of Big School
they stick to easy favourites – primary colours primed and ready
until with *Turquoise*, the treasures emerge: *Teal* Miss! *Cyan*
Magenta a breath before *Pearlescent Blue* – vowels and sounds
saved up like stones and shells and bits of broken mirror.

Roadworks

Crossroads maypoled with orange cones,
the stalled cars wind round them like ribbons.

You marvel at the gala of diggers, loaders,
dumpers, rollers, at the world being unfurled

before you. The drivers swing into their cabs
like acrobats: the rest bury themselves in their hi-vis

coats and hats, made shy by the sudden attention.
Later, I sit through the flashing lights alone, surprised

to find they are all still here, expecting them
to have moved on like a summer fair the moment

we passed through, leaving only the churned up
earth, some withered grass, and a promise to return.

The Distributor

I *For want*

Conspicuous in its absence
from some bollard or abandoned
post, it lies prostrate on the path.

A recalcitrant sentry at the pedestrian
crossing, the turned black cap of it
is trimmed with the rust of maple leaves.

It is as out of place here as the single hoof
in the museum's glass cabinet, severed
hollowed, lacquered, shod and crowned

with silver, inscribed and dedicated
to a favourite horse, the one who *carried
me at Tel-El-Kebir* and that was their reward.

Flung across the path and into the ditch
it lies there, unblinking. A crowd of branches
angle for the space to look into its face,
count themselves lucky. Shrubs scratch the sclera
like last night's mascara and still it stares up
at a sky it's never seen before, wondering when
the sun will come out from behind the clouds
and overtake it, knowing things like that
are always closer than they appear.

III *Beyond this point*

The sky is worn and grey: a once-white polo shirt
wrung through, it threatens rain when I am drenched
with sweat. A trolley lies in a ditch, its worn castors
weathervanes pointing north–north–west. Stigmatised

you wait by the abandoned gate with the teacher.
A black poppy blooms from the hole in your grey
tights. When we turn for home, the rain spits
in our faces, the wind throws litter in our hair, so

I heave you up and over the trolley's righted frame
and with a storm-filled cry we push off down the hill,
a sodden blur of red and yellow, blue and green,
laughing like drains at the cars that stop to watch.

IV *The badger*

I know the swaddled shape of it, the rise
of rump that obscures for five steps more
or six his striped head, his picture-book snout.

It is an uncomfortable story – the traffic, my body
and yours and his – turned against a wall as hard
and weathered as an artery. I cannot keep you safe

from both. I promise to call for help and tell you –
when you ask me, after school – that they arrived
in a warm blue van, thanked us for our trouble

and carried him away. Not that the line went dead –
when they asked me *Is it still alive?* – in the time it took
his last imagined breath to stir the fallen leaves.

V *I would call them rock doves*

one in the middle of the road, its heart
torn out and scattered like the feathers
clinging to its bloodied ribs; the other,

perched tightly on the lamppost we will
soon walk underneath. Its clawed
toes clutch the metal neck, warn us

to look away, to turn back, to take
time with us – the pigeons you don't see:
following the moon that follows us to school.

VI *The hedgehog*

I cannot tell if it is breathing
this sod of mossy turf,
curled under with the lifting
and left to dry, as if lying here
doesn't tell me everything
I need to know
about this garden ornament
with knots for eyes, face carved
and smoothed to a soft point.
A one-woman wake, I sit by the road
and wait until it is time to leave
this small toy sold for conservation,
let slip from sleeping hands, fallen
somewhere I cannot follow.

VII *Dandelion girl*

Legs and arms growing like weeds
I find her at the side of road. She
is no lion-toothed girl, no timekeeper.

Late for school, locked out and lost,
her tender roots wrap around my hands
like fingers. Her yellow fear whitens

with the breath of every question, each reply
a seed, a sail, a parachute, until her head
is full of yearnings longing to disperse.

*   *   *

This page

Here –

I am giving it to you
to fill a picture frame or push
into the toes of wet boots
to balance a table or keep out
a draught

Here –

to tear apart for art or bookmarks
or to give purpose to a magnet
on a fridge, to make a shopping
list or to pick up crumbs, to top
with drops of nail polish or stripe
with fallen food

Here –

to light a fire or catch a spider
to keep count, keep score, to fold
in four and tuck away because love
can be hard to hold. Whatever you use
this love for, use it. I am giving it to you

Here –

NOTES

The back of five: II (43)

'*eternal twilight*': from *The Planets* (BBC Two), presented by Professor Brian Cox, series 1, episode 1: *A Moment in the Sun – The Terrestrial Planets.*

The Distributor (53):

The local name given to the A8082 Southern Distributor Road in Inverness, Scotland.